Air Fryer Cookbook for One

Easy to make, Healthy and Delicious Air Fryer Recipes for Beginners

TASHA MANN

TABLE OF CONTENTS

Introduction

With technology giving birth to different and unique inventions every day to satisfy the hunger for innovation in society, the everyday kitchen's modernization is also seen. Among the many devices that have made life more comfortable with their usefulness and design, the Air Fryer is an excellent tool with many benefits.

An Air Fryer is a device that cooks food not by using oil but by heated air with no compromise on the dish's texture and flavor. Air Fryer is not only used for frying up food, but can also be used for many other tasks such as grilling, baking, roasting, and many more. It ensures the food is cooked evenly and thoroughly. Its design is such that it fits in a compact area and works via electricity. It has many different parts:

The frying basket: It is a stainless-steel basket in which the food is placed for cooking. It can be replaced by any other utensils, such as a pizza pan.

The timer: The timer is set accordingly; a red light indicates when the time has been finished.

The temperature controller: The temperature of the Air Fryer has a high range from 175 to 400F. Adjust the temp knob to achieve the desired temperature.

The air inlet/outlet: It is used to release the hot air and steam that arises during the cooking process from the device's back. It is, therefore, important that the device is always kept in a spacious area.

How to Start Cooking in An Air Fryer?

Firstly, the Air Fryer must be in a spacious place to allow heat to escape and prevent damage to its parts. It should be put on top of a heat resistance surface.

Secondly, pull out the frying basket gently from the machine. It is recommended to preheat the device for 5 minutes before using it. Simply set the desired temperature for 5 mins and then after the time is completed, pull out the basket.

Now place the food inside the container. Not more than 2/3 of the container should be filled. If required, the container can be greased with an oil spray to avoid sticking the food. If fatty foods are placed, add a little bit of water so that the container remains clean.

CHAPTER 1

Breakfast

1.   Gourmet Cheesy Bread

Basic Recipe

Preparation Time: 10 minutes

Cooking Time: 15 minutes

Servings: 2

Ingredients:

1 tablespoon of olives

1 tablespoon of mustard

1 tablespoon of paprika

3 bread slices

2 tablespoons of cheddar cheese

2 eggs, whites and yolks, separated

1 tablespoon of chives

Directions:

Arrange the bread slices in the cooking tray. Set the Instant Vortex on Air fryer to 355 degrees F for 5 minutes. Insert the cooking tray in the Vortex when it displays "Add Food". Remove from the oven when cooking time is complete. Whisk thoroughly egg whites in a bowl and fold in the cheese, egg yolks, paprika, and mustard. Spread this mixture over the bread slices and place in the cooking tray. Cook again in the vortex for about 10 minutes and dish out to serve.

Nutrition:

Calories: 164 Protein: 10.2g

Carbs: 11.1g Fat: 9.2g

2.   Crust Less Quiche

Preparation Time: 2 minutes

Cooking Time: 25 minutes

Servings: 6

Ingredients:

½ cup of milk

1 cup of Gouda cheese, shredded

4 eggs

¼ cup of onion, chopped

½ cup of tomatoes, chopped

Salt, to taste

Directions:

Combine all the ingredients into 2 greased ramekins and place them on the cooking tray. Set the Instant Vortex on Air fryer to 340 degrees F for 25 minutes. Insert the cooking tray in the Vortex when it displays "Add Food". Remove from the oven when cooking time is complete.

Serve warm.

Nutrition:

Calories: 348

Protein: 26.1g

Carbs: 7.9g

Fat: 23.1g

3.　**Breakfast Creamy Donuts**

Preparation Time: 10 minutes

Cooking Time: 8 minutes

Servings: 8

Ingredients:

3 medium red bell peppers, remove and discard seeds, slice

into quarters

Nonstick cooking spray

1 medium onion, sliced into 1/2-inch slices

1½ teaspoons of baking powder

1 pinch of baking soda

1/3 cup of caster sugar

1 teaspoon of cinnamon

½ cup of sugar

4 tablespoons of butter, softened and divided

2 large egg yolks

2¼ cups of plain flour

1 teaspoon salt

½ cup of sour cream

Directions:

Cream together sugar, egg yolks, and butter in a bowl. Strain together flour, baking powder, baking soda and salt in another bowl. Fold in the creamed sugar mixture and sour cream to form a dough. Slice the dough in half and roll into 2-inch thickness. Drizzle melted butter over both sides of the dough and move in the cooking tray. Set the Instant Vortex on Air fryer to 365 degrees F for 8 minutes. Insert the cooking tray in the Vortex when it displays "Add Food". Remove from the oven when cooking time is complete. Serve sprinkled with the cinnamon and caster sugar.

Nutrition :

Calories 303 Protein 4.8g

Carbs 49.1g

Fat: 10.2g

4.　Mixed Scrambled Eggs

Preparation Time: 10 minutes

Cooking Time: 10 minutes

Servings:　2

Ingredients:

8 grape tomatoes, halved

½ cup of Parmesan cheese, grated

¾ cup of milk

1 tablespoon of butter

Salt and black pepper, to taste

4 eggs

Directions:

Whip the eggs with milk, salt, and black pepper in a bowl. Pour the egg mixture into the cooking tray along with the grape tomatoes and cheese. Set the Instant Vortex on Air fryer to 360 degrees F for 10 minutes. Insert the cooking tray in the Vortex when it displays "Add Food". Remove from the

oven when cooking time is complete. Serve warm.

Nutrition :

Calories 351

Protein 26.4g

Carbs 25.2g Fat: 22g

5. Toast Less Sausage in Egg Pond

Preparation Time: 20 minutes

Cooking Time: 20 minutes

Servings: 4

Ingredients:

1 bread slice, cut into sticks

3 eggs

2 cooked sausages, sliced

1/8 cup of Parmesan cheese, grated

¼ cup of cream

1/8 cup of mozzarella cheese, grated

Directions:

Whip the eggs with cream in a bowl. Pour the egg mixture into the ramekins and fold in the sausage and bread slices. Place the ramekins in the cooking tray. Set the Instant Vortex on Air fryer to 365 degrees F for 20 minutes. Insert the cooking tray in the Vortex when it displays "Add Food".

Remove from the oven when cooking time is complete. Serve warm.

Nutrition :

Calories 26 Protein 18.3g Carbs 4.2g

Fat 18.8g

6.   Vegetable Quiche

Preparation Time: 10 minutes

Cooking Time: 24 minutes

Servings: 6

Ingredients:

8 eggs

1 cup coconut milk

1 cup tomatoes, chopped

1 cup zucchini, chopped

1 tbsp. butter

1 onion, chopped

1 cup Parmesan cheese, grated

1/2 tsp. pepper

1 tsp. salt

Directions:

Preheat the air fryer to 370 F.

Melt butter in a pan over medium heat then add onion and sauté until onion lightly brown.

Add tomatoes and zucchini to the pan and sauté for 4-5 minutes.

Transfer cooked vegetables into the air fryer baking dish.

Beat eggs with cheese, milk, pepper, and salt in a bowl.

Pour egg mixture over vegetables in a baking dish.

Place dish in the air fryer and cook for 24 minutes or until eggs are set.

Slice and serve.

Nutrition:

Calories 255

Fat 16 g

Carbohydrates 8 g

Sugar 4.2 g

Protein 21 g

Cholesterol 257 mg

7.   Breakfast Egg Tomato

Preparation Time: 10 minutes

Cooking Time: 24 minutes

Servings: 2

Ingredients:

2 eggs

2 large fresh tomatoes

1 tsp. fresh parsley

Pepper

Salt

Directions:

Preheat the air fryer to 325 F.

Cut off the top of a tomato and spoon out the tomato innards.

Break the egg in each tomato and place in air fryer basket and cook for 24 minutes.

Season with parsley, pepper, and salt.

Serve and enjoy.

Nutrition:

Calories 95

Fat 5 g

Carbohydrates 7.5 g

Sugar 5.1 g

Protein 7 g

Cholesterol 164 mg

CHAPTER 2

Mains

8.   Pesto Tomatoes

Preparation Time: 5 minutes

Cooking Time:14 minutes

Servings:4

Ingredients:

Large heirloom tomatoes – 3, cut into ½ inch thick slices.

1 cup pesto 8 oz feta cheese, cut into ½ inch thick slices

½ cup red onion, sliced thinly 1 tablespoon olive oil

Directions:

Spread some pesto on each slice of tomato.Top each tomato

slice with a feta slice and onion and drizzle with oil. Arrange the tomatoes onto the greased rack and spray with cooking spray. Arrange the drip pan in the bottom of the Instant Vortex Air Fryer Oven cooking chamber. Select "Air Fry" and then adjust the temperature to 390 °F. Set the time for 14 minutes and press "Start". When the display shows "Add Food" insert the rack in the center position. When the display shows "Turn Food" do not turn food. When cooking time is complete, remove the rack from the Vortex Oven.Serve warm.

Nutrition:

Calories 480

Carbs 13g

Fat 41.9g

Protein 15.4g

9.　　Herbed Potatoes

Preparation Time: 5 minutes

Cooking Time:20 minutes

Servings:4

Ingredients:

1 lb small red potatoes, cut into 1-inch pieces

1 tablespoon olive oil

1 teaspoon chopped fresh thyme

1 teaspoon chopped fresh rosemary

1 teaspoon chopped fresh oregano

salt and ground black pepper, as required

1 tablespoon grate lemon zest

Directions:

In a bowl, add all ingredients except lemon zest and toss to coat well. Place the potatoes in the rotisserie basket and attach the lid.

Arrange the drip pan in the bottom of the Instant Vortex Air Fryer Oven cooking chamber. Select "Air Fry" and then adjust the temperature to 400 °F. Set the time for 20 minutes and press "Start". Then, close the door and touch "Rotate". When the display shows "Add Food" arrange the rotisserie basket, on the rotisserie spit. Then, close the door and touch "Rotate". When cooking time is complete, press the red lever to release the rod. Remove from the Vortex and transfer the potatoes into a bowl. Add the lemon zest and toss to coat well. Serve immediately.

Nutrition:

Calories 112

Carbs 18.7g

Fat 3.7g

Protein 2.2g

10.   Seasoned Potatoes

Preparation Time: 10 minutes

Cooking Time:40 minutes

Servings:1

Ingredients:

2 russet potatoes, scrubbed

½ tablespoon butter, melted

½ teaspoon garlic & herb blend seasoning

½ teaspoon garlic powder

Salt, as required

Directions:

In a small bowl, mix together spices and salt. With a fork, prick the potatoes. Coat the potatoes with butter and sprinkle with spice mixture. Arrange the potatoes onto the cooking rack. Arrange the drip pan in the bottom of the Instant Vortex Air Fryer Oven cooking chamber. Select "Air Fry" and then adjust the temperature to 400 °F. Set the time for 40 minutes and press "Start". When the display shows "Add Food" insert the cooking rack in the center position. When the display shows "Turn Food" do nothing. When cooking time is complete, remove the tray from the Vortex Oven. Serve hot.

Nutrition:

Calories 176

Carbs 34.2g

Fat 2.1g

Protein 3.8g

11.　Rich Beef and Sausage Meatloaf

Preparation Time: 15 minutes

Cooking Time:25 minutes

Servings:4

Ingredients:

3/4-pound ground chuck

1/4 pound ground pork sausage

1 cup shallot, finely chopped

2 eggs, well beaten

3 tablespoons plain milk

1 tablespoon oyster sauce

1 teaspoon porcini mushrooms

1/2 teaspoon cumin powder

1 teaspoon garlic paste

1 tablespoon fresh parsley

Seasoned salt and crushed red pepper flakes, to taste

1 cup parmesan cheese, grated

Directions:

Simply place all ingredients in a large-sized mixing dish; mix until everything is thoroughly combined.

Press the meatloaf mixture into the Air Fryer baking dish; set your Air Fryer to cook at 360 degrees F for 25 minutes. Press the power button and cook until heated through.

Check for doneness and serve with your favorite wine!

Nutrition:

206 Calories

7.9g Fat

15.9g Carbs

17.6g Protein

0.8g Sugars

0.4g Fiber

12. Japanese Miso Steak

Preparation Time: 1 hour

Cooking Time:15 minutes

Servings:4

Ingredients:

1 ¼ pounds flank steak

1 ½ tablespoons sake

1 tablespoon brown miso paste

2 garlic cloves, pressed

1 tablespoon olive oil

Directions:

Place all the ingredients in a sealable food bag; shakeuntil completely coated and place in your refrigerator for at least 1 hour.

Then, spritz the steak with a non-stick cooking spray; make sure to coat on all sides. Place the steak in the Air Fryer baking pan.

Set your Air Fryer to cook at 400 degrees F. Roast for 12 minutes, flipping twice. Serve immediately.

Nutrition:

367 Calories

15.1g Fat

6.4g Carbs

48.6g Protein

3.4g Sugars

0.3g Fiber

CHAPTER 3

Sides

13.   Cheddar, Squash 'n Zucchini Casserole

Preparation Time: 10 minutes

Cooking Time:30 minutes

Servings:4

Ingredients:

1 egg

5 saltine crackers, or as needed, crushed

2 tablespoons bread crumbs

1/2-pound yellow squash, sliced

1/2-pound zucchini, sliced

1/2 cup shredded Cheddar cheese

1-1/2 teaspoons white sugar

1/2 teaspoon salt

1/4 onion, diced

1/4 cup biscuit baking mix

1/4 cup butter

Directions:

Lightly grease baking pan of air fryer with cooking spray. Add onion, zucchini, and yellow squash. Cover pan with foil and for 15 minutes, cook on 360oF or until tender. Stir in salt, sugar, egg, butter, baking mix, and cheddar cheese. Mix well. Fold in crushed crackers. Top with bread crumbs. Cook for 15 minutes at 390oF until tops are lightly browned. Serve and enjoy.

Nutrition:Calories 285Carbs 16.4g

Protein 8.6gFat 20.5g

14.   Cheesy Spinach

Preparation Time: 5 minutes

Cooking Time: 15 minutes

Servings: 3

Ingredients:

Frozen spinach – 1 (10-oz.) Package, thawed

½ cup onion, chopped

2 teaspoon minced garlic

4 oz cream cheese. Chopped

½ teaspoon ground nutmeg

Salt and ground black pepper, as required

¼ cup parmesan cheese, shredded

Directions:

In a bowl, mix together spinach, onion, garlic, cream cheese, nutmeg, salt, and black pepper. Place the spinach mixture into a baking dish that will fit in the Vortex Air Fryer Oven. Arrange the drip pan in the bottom of the Instant Vortex Air

Fryer Oven cooking chamber. Select "Air Fry" and then adjust the temperature to 355 °F. Set the time for 15 minutes and press "Start". When the display shows "Add Food" insert the baking dish in the center position. When the display shows "Turn Food" do not turn food. When cooking time is complete, remove the baking dish from the Vortex Oven. Serve hot.

Nutrition:

Calories 194

Carbs 7.3g

Fat 15.5g

Protein 8.4g

15.   Spicy Zucchini

Preparation Time: 10 minutes

Cooking Time:12 minutes

Servings:3

Ingredients:

Zucchini – 1 lb. Cut into ½-inch thick slices lengthwise

1 tablespoon olive oil

½ teaspoon garlic powder

½ teaspoon cayenne pepper

Salt and ground black pepper, as required

Directions:

Add all the ingredients into a bowl and toss to coat well.

Arrange the zucchini slices onto a cooking tray.

Arrange the drip pan in the bottom of the Instant Vortex Air Fryer Oven cooking chamber. Select "Air Fry" and then adjust the temperature to 400 °F. Set the time for 12 minutes and press "Start".

When the display shows "Add Food" insert the cooking tray in the center position. When the display shows "Turn Food" do nothing. When cooking time is complete, remove the tray from the Vortex Oven. Serve hot.

Nutrition:

Calories 67

Carbs 5.6g

Fat 5g

Protein 2g

16. Seasoned Yellow Squash

Preparation Time: 5 minutes

Cooking Time:6 minutes

Servings:2

Ingredients:

4 large yellow squash, cut into slices

¼ cup olive oil

½ onion, sliced

¾ teaspoon italian seasoning

½ teaspoon garlic salt

¼ teaspoon seasoned salt

Directions:

In a large bowl, mix together all the ingredients. Place the veggie mixture in the greased cooking tray.

Arrange the drip pan in the bottom of Instant Vortex Air Fryer Oven cooking chamber. Select "Air Fry" and then adjust the temperature to 400 °F.

Set the time for 10 minutes and press "Start". When the display shows "Add Food" insert the cooking tray in the center position.

When the display shows "Turn Food" turn the vegetables. When cooking time is complete, remove the tray from the Vortex Oven. Serve hot.

Nutrition:

Calories 113

Carbs 8.1g

Fat 9g

Protein 4.2g

17. Buttered Asparagus

Preparation Time: 5 minutes

Cooking Time:10 minutes

Servings:3

Ingredients:

1 lb. trimmed Fresh thick asparagus spears

1 tablespoon melted Butter

Salt and ground black pepper, as required

Directions:

Add all the ingredients into a bowl and toss to coat well. Arrange the asparagus onto a cooking tray. Arrange the drip pan in the bottom of Instant Vortex Air Fryer Oven cooking chamber. Select "Air Fry" and then adjust the temperature to 350 °F. Set the time for 10 minutes and press "Start". When the display shows "Add Food" insert the cooking tray in the center position. When the display shows "Turn Food" turn the asparagus. When cooking time is complete, remove the tray from Vortex Oven. Serve hot.

Nutrition:

Calories 64 Carbs 5.9g

Fat 4g Protein 3.4g

18. Balsamic Brussels Sprouts

Preparation Time: 10 minutes

Cooking Time:20 minutes

Servings:4

Ingredients:

Brussels sprouts – 1 lb. Ends trimmed and cut into bite-sized

pieces

1 tablespoon balsamic vinegar

1 tablespoon olive oil

Salt and ground black pepper, as required

Directions:

Add all the ingredients into a bowl and toss to coat well. Place

the Brussels Sprouts in the rotisserie basket and attach the lid.

Arrange the drip pan in the bottom of Instant Vortex Air

Fryer Oven cooking chamber. Select "Air Fry" and then

adjust the temperature to 350 °F. Set the time for 20 minutes

and press "Start". Then, close the door and touch "Rotate".

When the display shows "Add Food" arrange the rotisserie basket, on the rotisserie spit. Then, close the door and touch "Rotate". When cooking time is complete, press the red lever to release the rod. Remove from the Vortex Oven. Serve hot.

Nutrition:

Calories 80

Carbs 10.3g

Fat 3.9g

Protein 3.9g

19. Parmesan Broccoli

Preparation Time: 5 minutes

Cooking Time:6 minutes

Servings:4

Ingredients:

1 lb. small broccoli florets

1 tablespoon minced garlic

2 tbsps. olive oil

¼ cup parmesan cheese, grated

Directions:

Add all the ingredients into a bowl and toss to coat well.

Arrange the broccoli florets onto a cooking tray.

Arrange the drip pan in the bottom of the Instant Vortex Air

Fryer Oven cooking chamber. Select "Air Fry" and then

adjust the temperature to 350 °F.

Set the time for 6 minutes and press "Start". When the display shows "Add Food" insert the cooking tray in the center position.

When the display shows "Turn Food" turn the broccoli florets. When cooking time is complete, remove the tray from Vortex Oven.

Serve hot.

Nutrition:

Calories 112

Carbs 18.7g

Fat 3.7g

Protein 2.2g

20.   Buttered Broccoli

Preparation Time: 5 minutes

Cooking Time:15 minutes

Servings:4

Ingredients:

1 lb. broccoli florets

1 tablespoon melted butter

½ teaspoon crushed red pepper flakes

Salt and ground black pepper, as required

Directions:

Add all the ingredients into a bowl and toss to coat well. Place the broccoli florets in the rotisserie basket and attach the lid. Arrange the drip pan in the bottom of the Instant Vortex Air Fryer Oven cooking chamber. Select "Air Fry" and then adjust the temperature to 400 °F. Set the time for 15 minutes and press "Start".

Then, close the door and touch "Rotate". When the display shows "Add Food" arrange the rotisserie basket, on the rotisserie spit. Then, close the door and touch "Rotate". When cooking time is complete, press the red lever to release the rod. Remove from the Vortex Oven. Serve immediately.

Nutrition:

Calories 55

Carbs 6.1g

Fat 3g

Protein 2.3g

CHAPTER 4

Fish and Seafood

21.   Herb Salmon Fillet

Preparation Time: 2 minutes

Cooking Time: 8 minutes

Servings: 2

Ingredients:

½ lb. salmon fillet

¼ tsp thyme

1 tsp garlic powder

½ tsp cayenne pepper

½ tsp paprika

¼ tsp sage

¼ tsp oregano

salt and pepper to taste

Directions:

Rub the seasoning all over the salmon. Preheat your air fryer to 350°Fahrenheit. Place the seasoned salmon fillet into an air fryer basket and cook for 8-minutes.

Nutrition:

Calories 298

 Fat 9.3g,

Carbs 8.6g,

Protein10.2g

22.   Crunchy Fish Taco

Preparation Time: 5 minutes

Cooking Time: 18 minutes

Servings: 4

Ingredients:

12-ounce cod fillet

Salt and black pepper to taste

1 cup tempura batter

1 cup breadcrumbs

½ cup guacamole

6-flour tortillas

2 tbsp cilantro, freshly chopped

½ cup of salsa

1 lemon, juiced

Directions:

Cut the cod fillets lengthwise into 2-inch pieces and season it

with pepper and salt. Dip each cod strip into tempura butter then into breadcrumbs. Preheat your air fryer to 340°Fahrenheit and cook cod for 13-minutes. Spread guacamole on each tortilla. Place cod stick on tortilla and top with chopped cilantro and salsa. Squeeze lemon juice on top, then fold and serve.

Nutrition:

Calories 300

Fat 10.3g

Carbs 8.9g

Protein 14.8g

23.   Air-Fryer Baked Salmon & Asparagus

Preparation Time: 5 minutes

Cooking Time: 15 minutes

Servings: 4

Ingredients:

4 salmon fillets

 4asparagus

2 tsp butter

3 lemons, sliced

salt and pepper to taste

Directions:

Preheat the air fryer to 300°Fahrenheit. Take four pieces of aluminum foil. Add asparagus, half lemon juice, pepper, and salt in a bowl and toss. Divide seasoned asparagus evenly on four aluminum foil pieces. Put one salmon fillet asparagus. Put some lemon slices on top of salmon fillets. Fold foil tightly to seal the parcel. Place in an air fryer basket and cook

for 15-minutes. Serve warm.

Nutrition:

Calories 291

Fat 16g

Carbs 1g

Protein 35g

24. Potato Fish Cake

Preparation Time: 10 minutes

Cooking Time: 15 minutes

Servings: 2

Ingredients:

1 ½ cups white fish, cooked

pepper and salt to taste 1 ½ tbsp of milk

½ cup of mashed potatoes 1 tbsp butter

2 tsp gluten-free flour 1 tsp parsley

½ tsp sage

Directions:

Add ingredients to a mixing bowl and combine well. Make round patties and place them in the fridge for 1 hour. Place the patties into the air fryer at 375°Fahrenheit for 15-minutes.

Nutrition:

Calories 167 Fat 9g

Carbs 14g, Protein 5g

CHAPTER 5

Poultry

25.   Turkey, Mushrooms and Peas Casserole

Preparation Time: 10 minutes

Cooking Time: 20 minutes

Servings: 4

Ingredients:

2 lbs. turkey breasts, skinless, boneless

1 yellow onion, chopped

1 celery stalk, chopped.

1/2 cup peas

1 cup chicken stock

1 cup cream, mushrooms soup

1 cup bread cubes

Salt and black pepper

Directions:

In a pan that fits your air fryer oven, mix turkey with salt, pepper, onion, celery, peas and stock, introduce in your air fryer oven and cook at 360 °F for 15 minutes.

Add bread cubes and cream of mushroom soup; stir toss and cook at 360 °F for 5 minutes more.

Divide among plates and serve hot.

Nutrition:

Calories 271

Fats 9 g

Carbs 16 g

Proteins 7 g

26.   Duck Breasts with Red Wine and Orange Sauce

Preparation Time: 10 minutes

Cooking Time: 27 minutes Servings: 4

Ingredients:

2 duck breasts, skin on and halved

2 cups chicken stock

2 cups orange juice

2 tsp. pumpkin pie spice

2 tbsp. olive oil

2 tbsp. butter

1/2 cup honey

2 tbsp. sherry vinegar

4 cups red wine Salt and black pepper

Directions:

Heat up a pan with the orange juice over medium heat, add honey stir well and cook for 10 minutes.

Add wine, vinegar, stock, pie spice and butter stir well, cook for 10 minutes more and take off heat.

Season duck breasts with salt and pepper, rub with olive oil, place in preheated air fryer oven at 370 °F and cook for 7 minutes on each side.

Divide duck breasts on plates, drizzle wine and orange juice all over and serve right away.

Nutrition:

Calories 300

Fats 8g

Carbs 24g

Proteins 11g

27. Coconut Creamy Chicken

Preparation:5 minutes Cooking: 25 minutesServings: 4

Ingredients:

4 big chicken legs

5 tsp. turmeric powder

2 tbsp. ginger, grated 4 tbsp. coconut cream

Salt and black pepper

Directions:

In a bowl, mix cream with turmeric, ginger, salt and pepper, whisk, add chicken pieces, toss them well and leave aside for 2 hours.

Transfer chicken to your preheated air fryer oven, cook at 370 °F for 25 minutes; divide among plates and serve with a side salad.

Nutrition:

Calories 300 Fats 4g Carbs 22g

Proteins 20g

CHAPTER 6

Meat

28.   Mexican Chorizo & Beef Empanadas

Preparation Time: 10 minutes

Cooking Time: 35 minutes Servings: 4

Ingredients:

2 garlic cloves, minced

½ cup green bell pepper, chopped

1 red onion, chopped

4 oz. chorizo, chopped

½ pound ground beef

4 dough discs

1 cup Mexican blend cheese, shredded

2 tbsp. vegetable oil

¼ cup chunky salsa

Salt and black pepper to taste

Directions:

Heat the vegetable oil in a pan over medium heat and sauté bell pepper, garlic, and onion for 4 minutes until tender. Add the ground beef and chorizo, and stir-fry for 5-6 minutes. Season it with pepper and salt. Pour in chunky salsa and cook, stirring occasionally, until the sauce thickens, 5 minutes. Preheat the air fryer to 390 F. Divide the meat mixture and cheese between the dough discs. Fold them in half over the filling; press and seal the edges with a fork. Spritz with cooking spray and transfer to the air fryer basket. Bake for 12-15 minutes, turning once until golden. Let cool slightly before serving.

Nutrition: Calories 322 Fat 12.5g

Protein 7.1g

29.   Beef Roast with Red Potatoes

Preparation Time: 15 minutes

Cooking Time: 50 minutes

Servings: 4

Ingredients:

2 tbsp. olive oil

2-pound top round roast beef

salt and black pepper to taste

½ tsp. dried thyme

1 tsp. fresh rosemary, chopped

1 pound red potatoes, halved

Directions:

Preheat the air fryer to 360 F. In a bowl, mix rosemary, salt, pepper, 1 tbsp. of olive oil, and thyme; rub onto the beef. Place the meat in the frying basket and Bake for 15-18 minutes. Give the meat a turn and cook for 10 more minutes. Remove the steak to a plate, cover with foil to keep warm.

Season the potatoes with the remaining olive oil, salt, and pepper, and Bake in the air fryer for 25 minutes at 400 F. Slice the beef and serve with potatoes.

Nutrition:

Calories 313.5

Fat 6.9g

Protein 5.8g

30. Beef Veggie Mix with Hoisin Sauce

Preparation Time: 10 minutes

Cooking Time: 55 minutes

Servings: 4

Ingredients:

Hoisin Sauce:

2 tbsp. soy sauce

1 tbsp. peanut butter

½ tsp. sriracha sauce

1 tsp. sugar

1 tsp. rice vinegar

3 cloves garlic, minced

Beef Veggie Mix:

2 lb. beef sirloin steak, cut into strips

2 yellow peppers, cut into strips

2 green peppers cut into strips

2 white onions cut into strips

1 red onion, cut into strips

2 lb. broccoli cut in florets

2 tbsp. soy sauce

2 tsp. sesame oil

3 tsp. minced garlic

2 tsp. ground ginger

1 tbsp. olive oil

Directions:

Place a pan over low heat and add all the hoisin sauce ingredients. Bring to a simmer and cook until reduced, for about 3-4 minutes. Stir occasionally using a vessel and then let cool. To the chilled hoisin sauce, add garlic, sesame oil, soy sauce, ginger, and ½ cup of water; mix well. Stir in the beef, cover, and refrigerate for 20 minutes to marinade. In a greased baking dish, combine broccoli, peppers, onions, and olive oil. Place the dish in the fryer. Bake for 10 minutes at 400 F, shaking once. Transfer to a plate and cover with foil to keep warm. Remove the meat from the fridge and drain the liquid into a bowl. Add the beef into the fryer and Bake at 380 F for 10 minutes, shake, and cook for 7 more minutes. Transfer to the veggie plate, season it with pepper and salt, and pour the hoisin sauce over. Serve immediately.

Nutrition:

Calories 315.5

Fat 7.1g

Protein 7.3g

31.   Mexican Beef Cabbage Wraps

Preparation Time: 15 minutes

Cooking Time: 30 minutes

Servings: 4

Ingredients:

1 lb. ground beef

8 savoy cabbage leaves

1 small onion, chopped

1 tsp. taco seasoning

1 tbsp. cilantro-lime rotel

⅔ cup Mexican cheese, shredded

2 tbsp. olive oil

salt and black pepper to taste

2 garlic cloves, minced1 tbsp. fresh cilantro, chopped

Directions:

Preheat the air fryer to 400 F. Heat olive oil in a skillet over

medium heat and sauté onion and garlic until fragrant, about

3 minutes. Add in ground beef, salt, black pepper, and taco seasoning. Cook until the beef browns while breaking it with a vessel as it cooks. Add cilantro rotel and stir to combine. Lay 4 savoy cabbage leaves on a flat surface and scoop ¼ of the beef mixture in the center; sprinkle with Mexican cheese. Wrap diagonally and double wrap with the remaining cabbage leaves. Arrange the rolls on the greased air fryer basket and Bake for 8 minutes. Flip the rolls and cook for 5 more minutes. Remove to a plate, garnish with cilantro and let cool before serving.

Nutrition:

Calories 425.1 Fat 7.5g Protein 5.6g

32.   Chimichurri New York Steak

Preparation Time: 5 minutes

Cooking Time: 20 minutes

Servings: 4

Ingredients:

½ cup chimichurri salsa

2 tbsp. olive oil

1 New York strip steak

1 tbsp. smoked paprika

Sea salt and black pepper to taste

1 jar (16-oz) roasted peppers, sliced

Directions:

Preheat the air fryer to 380 F. Grease the air fryer basket with

cooking spray. Rub the steak with smoked paprika, sea salt,

and pepper. Drizzle with olive oil and Bake in the air fryer for

12-14 minutes, turning once halfway through. Transfer to a

cutting board and let it sit for a few minutes. Slice, drizzle the chimichurri salsa, and serve immediately with roasted peppers.

Nutrition:

Calories 435.6

Fat 12.4g

Protein 8g

CHAPTER 7

Vegetables

33. Creamy Brussels Sprouts

Preparation Time: 10 minutes

Cooking Time: 25 minutes

Servings: 8

Ingredients:

3 lbs. brussels sprouts, halved

A drizzle of olive oil

1 lbs.bacon, chopped

salt and black pepper to the taste

4 tbsp. butter

3 shallots, chopped

1 cup milk

2 cups heavy cream

¼ tsp. nutmeg, ground

3 tbsp. horseradish

Directions:

Preheat your air fryer at 370 degrees F, add oil, bacon, salt and pepper and Brussels sprouts and toss. Add butter, shallots, heavy cream, milk, nutmeg and horseradish, toss again and cook for 25 minutes. Divide among plates and serve as a side dish. Enjoy!

Nutrition:

Calories 214

Fat 5

Protein 5

34.   Cheddar Biscuits

Preparation Time: 10 minutes

Cooking Time: 20 minutes

Servings: 8

Ingredients:

2 and 1/3 cup self-rising flour

½ cup butter 1 tbsp., melted

2 tbsp. sugar

½ cup cheddar cheese, grated

1 and 1/3 cup buttermilk

1 cup flour

Directions:

In a bowl, mix self-rising flour with ½ cup butter, sugar, cheddar cheese and buttermilk and stir until you obtain a dough. Spread 1 cup flour on a working surface, roll dough, flatten it, cut 8 circles with a cookie cutter and coat them with flour. Line your air fryer's basket with tin foil, add biscuits, brush them with melted butter and cook them at 380 degrees

F for 20 minutes. Divide among plates and serve as a side.

Enjoy!

Nutrition:

Calories 221

Fat 3

Protein 4

35. Herbed Tomatoes

Preparation Time: 10 minutes

Cooking Time: 15 minutes Servings: 4

Ingredients:

4 big tomatoes, halved and insides scooped out

salt and black pepper to the taste

1 tbsp. olive oil

2 garlic cloves, minced

½ tsp. thyme, chopped

Directions:

In your air fryer, mix tomatoes with salt, pepper, oil, garlic and thyme, toss and cook at 390 degrees F for 15 minutes. Divide among plates and serve them as a side dish. Enjoy!

Nutrition:

Calories 112

Fat 1g

Protein 4g

36. Roasted Peppers

Preparation: 10 minutes Cooking: 20 minutes

Servings: 4

Ingredients:

1 tbsp. sweet paprika 1 tbsp. olive oil

4 red bell peppers, cut into medium strips

4 green bell peppers, cut into medium strips

4 yellow bell peppers, cut into medium strips

1 yellow onion, chopped

salt and black pepper to the taste

Directions:

In your air fryer, mix red bell peppers with green and yellow ones. Add paprika, oil, onion, salt and pepper, toss and cook at 350 degrees F for 20 minutes. Divide among plates and serve as a side dish. Enjoy.

Nutrition: Calories 142 Fat 4 Protein 4

CHAPTER 8

Soup and Stews

37.   Fast Bean Stew

Preparation Time: 10 minutes

Cooking Time: 25 minutes Servings: 4

Ingredients:

1 garlic head, halved

2 carrots, peeled and chopped

1 pound chickpeas, drained

1 teaspoon dried oregano

3 bay leaves

22 ounces canned diced tomatoes

22 ounces water

2 tablespoons olive oil

½ teaspoon red pepper flakes

Olive oil, for serving

2 tablespoons Parmesan cheese, grated

Salt and ground black pepper, to taste

Directions:

Place the onion, carrot, garlic, chickpeas, tomato, water, oregano, bay leaf, 2 tablespoons of oil, salt and pepper in the Air fryer.

Cover, cook in the Meat / Stew setting for 25 minutes and release the pressure. Pour into bowls, add cheese, pepper flakes and a drizzle of oil and serve.

Nutrition:

Calories164, Fat 2, Fiber: 9, Carbohydrate: 28, Proteins: 8.2

CHAPTER 9

Snacks

38.   Frozen Pizza

Preparation Time: 5 minutes

Cooking Time: 15-30 minutes Servings: 1

Ingredients:

1 piece Frozen Pizza

Directions:

Cook for 20 minutes at 1800C turning after 15 minutes.

Nutrition:

Calories 576 Fat 26g Carbohydrates 62g

Sugars 7.7g Protein 22g Cholesterol 30mg

39. Roasted Almonds

Preparation: 5 minutes Cooking: 8 minutes Servings: 8

Ingredients:

2 cups almonds

1/4 tsp pepper

1 tsp paprika

1 tbsp garlic powder

1 tbsp soy sauce

Directions:

Add pepper, paprika, garlic powder, and soy sauce in a bowl and stir well. Add almonds and stir to coat. Spray air fryer oven basket with cooking spray. Add almonds in air fryer oven basket and cook for 6-8 minutes at 320 F. Shake basket after every 2 minutes. Serve and enjoy.

Nutrition:

Calories 143 Fat 11.9 g Carbohydrates 6.2 g Sugar 1.3 g

Protein 5.4 g Cholesterol 0 mg

40. Two Ingredients Air Fryer Croutons

Preparation Time: 3 minutes

Cooking Time:8 minutes

Servings:9

Ingredients:

2 Slices

Whole meal Bread

1 tablespoon

Olive Oil

Directions:

Chop slices of bread into medium chunks and place in Air Fryer. Add olive oil and cook for 8 minutes on a 200c heat. Serve over soup or as a snack.

Nutrition:

Calories 30kcal Carbs 3g

Protein 0g Fat 1g Fiber 0g

Calcium 9mg

41. Air Fryer Strawberry Cupcakes

Preparation Time: 15 minutes

Cooking Time:8 minutes

Servings:10

Ingredients:

100 g Butter1

00 g Caster Sugar

2 Medium Eggs

100 g Self Raising Flour

½ teaspoon Vanilla Essence

50 g Butter

100 g Icing Sugar½ teaspoon

Pink Food Colouring

1 tablespoon Whipped Cream

¼ Cup Fresh Strawberries blended

Directions:

Preheat air fryer to 170c.

Cream butter and sugar in a large mixing bowl until light and fluffy; add vanilla essence and beat in eggs one at a time (adding little flour after each egg). Then fold in the rest of the flour.

Place them in little bun cases but don't fill the cases too much.

Place cupcakes in air fryer and cook for 8 minutes on 170c.

Meanwhile, cream butter and gradually add icing sugar until you have a creamy mixture, then add food colouring, whipped cream and blended strawberries and mix well.

Once the cupcakes are done, use a piping bag to add topping to them in circular motions

Serve and enjoy.

Nutrition:

Calories 236kcal

Carbs 27g

Protein 2g Fat 13g

Calcium 10mg

42.   Air Fryer Shortbread

Preparation Time: 10 minutes

Cooking Time:10 minutes

Servings:4

Ingredients:

250 g Self Raising Flour

175 g Butter

75 g Caster Sugar

Optional Ingredients:

30 g Cocoa Powder

Roses Chocolates

2 teaspoon Vanilla Essence

Chocolate Chips

Directions:

Place flour, butter and caster sugar in a bowl, rub butter into

flour until it resembles breadcrumbs then knead until you

have a dough ball

Roll out dough with rolling pin and cut into your favorite shapes using cookie cutters.

Use grill pan or baking mat inside your air fryer to cook dough. Set the temperature to 360f and cook for 10 minutes. Allow to cool before serving.

Nutrition:

Calories 635kcal

Carbs 69g

Protein 9g

Fat 38g

Saturated Fat 23g

Sodium 316mg

Fiber 4g

Sugar 19g

43. Air Fryer Mars Bar

Preparation Time: 10 minutes

Cooking Time:10 minutes

Servings:6

Ingredients:

225 g Self Raising Flour

100 g Butter

30 g Caster Sugar

6 Mars Bars

1 tablespoon Icing Sugar

Directions:

Place butter, caster sugar and self-rising flour in a mixing bowl, rub butter into the flour and sugar until it resembles breadcrumbs.

Add water to the breadcrumbs one bit at a time, while mixing until it forms a dough and knead until you have a soft pastry dough ball.

Roll out your pastry and cut into 6 similar sized pieces.

Roll each mars bar up in each of the six strips until the mars bar is not visible.

Place your mars bars into the air fryer, spacing them.

Cook for 6 minutes at 360f.

Sprinkle with icing sugar and serve.

Nutrition:

Calories 335kcal

Carbs 41g

Protein 5g

Fat 17g

Saturated Fat 10g

Cholesterol 37mg

Sodium 159mg

Potassium 58mg

Fiber 1g

CHAPTER 10

Desserts

44. Bean Stew Cookie

Preparation Time: 10 minutes

Cooking Time: 10-15 minutes

Servings: 2-4

Ingredients:

3 cups cooked and seasoned black beans or leftover beans with little broth.

6 tbsp cassava flour

2 tbsp of sour flour

Filling:

1 bunch of braised cabbage with cubes of bacon

To bread:

1 egg

2 cups panko flour, or toasted breadcrumbs.   Directions:

For the dough, beat the beans in a blender until it turns into a paste, or use a mixer. Pour the bean paste into a pan and add the yucca flour, stirring well until it turns into a smooth, well-cooked paste. Once warm, add the starch and mix well, set aside and allow cooling completely. To model, take pieces of dough, make a ball, open a dimple in the middle, put the chosen filling and close. After forming the bread, passing the slightly beaten egg and the chosen flour. Place half of the cookies in the Air Fryer basket and adjust for 10-15 minutes at 400°F.

Nutrition:

Calories 65.9

Fat 2.4g

Protein 1.7g

45.   Rolled Pizza

Preparation Time: 30 minutes

Cooking Time: 7 minutes Servings: 4

Ingredients:

Mass:

1 cup warm milk

1/3 cup warm water

¼ cup olive oil

2 tbsp of salt

2 tbsp of sugar

2 ½ tbsp of yeast

4 cups of flour

Filling:

½ lb of mozzarella cheese

3 ½ oz. of ham

1 ½ oz. of sliced olives

1/3 cup tomato sauce

oregano to taste Directions:

To Preparethe dough is very simple, simply mix all the Ingredients: in a bowl and knead well until you get homogeneous and smooth dough. Be careful not to add flour and make the dough hard, dry, or heavy. If you have a bread machine, just put everything inside the machine shape and set the kneading or dough cycle for at least 30 minutes, then remove and use the dough. Spread the dough out on a smooth rectangular surface, leaving it about 0.5 cm to 1 cm thick. Then add the cheese, the cold cuts, the sauce, the olives and the oregano and roll the dough wide, as shown in the photos below. The filling can be chopped or sliced. Cut the filled dough roll into slices 1.5 cm thick, then place these rolled slices in the Air Fryer basket and adjust for 7 minutes at 400°F. Do this with all the pizzas rolled up until you're done.

Nutrition: Calories 220 Fat 10g Protein 7g

46. Sequilho

Preparation Time: 5 minutes

Cooking Time: 10-12 minutes

Servings: 50

Ingredients

1 package of onion soup powder

2 cups of wheat flour

½ cup margarine or butter

1 egg

1 tbsp grated Parmesan cheese

2 tbsp of water

1 tbsp of baking powder

Directions:

In a bowl, put all the Ingredients: together and mix well, until it reaches the similar point of rotten, i.e., brittle, dough that is firm but not elastic and breaks slightly when squeezed. Roll the dough and squeeze with a fork to flatten and mark. Place half of the cookies in the Air Fryer basket and place them for 10 to 12 minutes at 400°F, they should be golden. Remove from the Air Fryer and allow to cool, place the other half of the cookies and repeat the process.

Once ready, before storage, after cold, they can be stored for up to 15 days in a closed container.

Nutrition:

Calories 53

Fat 2.04g

Protein 1.24g

47.   Honey-Roasted Pears with Ricotta

Preparation Time: 7 minutes

Cooking Time 18-23 minutes

Servings: 4

Ingredients:

2 large Bosc pears, halved lengthwise and seeded (see Tip)

3 tablespoons honey

1 tablespoon unsalted butter

½-teaspoon ground cinnamon

¼ cup walnuts, chopped

¼ cup part-skim ricotta cheese, divided

Directions:

Insert the crisper plate into the basket and the basket into the unit. Preheat the unit by selecting AIR ROAST, setting the temperature to 350°F, and setting the time to 3 minutes. Select START/STOP to begin. In a 6-by-2-inch round pan, place the pears cut-side up. In a small microwave-safe bowl, melt the honey, butter, and cinnamon. Brush this mixture over the cut sides of the pears.

Pour 3 tablespoons of water around the pears in the pan. Once the unit is preheated, place the pan into the basket. Select AIR ROAST, set the temperature to 350°F, and set the time to 23 minutes. Select START/STOP to begin. After about 18 minutes, check the pears. They should be tender when pierced with a fork and slightly crisp on the edges. If not, resume cooking.

When the cooking is complete, baste the pears once with the liquid in the pan. Carefully remove the pears from the pan and place on a serving plate. Drizzle each with some liquid from the pan, sprinkle the walnuts on top, and serve with a spoonful of ricotta cheese.

Nutrition:

Calories203 Fat 9g Carbohydrates: 30g Fiber: 4g

Protein4g

48.　Gooey Lemon Bars

Preparation Time: 15 minutes Cooking Time 25 minutes

Servings: 6

Ingredients:

¾ cup whole-wheat pastry flour 2 tablespoons confectioners'

sugar ¼ cup butter, melted

½ cup granulated sugar

1 tablespoon packed grated lemon zest (see Tip)

¼ cup freshly squeezed lemon juice

⅛ teaspoon sea salt

¼ cup unsweetened plain applesauce

2 teaspoons cornstarch

¾-teaspoon baking powder

Cooking oil spray (sunflower, safflower, or refined coconut)

Directions:

In a small bowl, stir together the flour, confectioners' sugar, and melted butter just until well combined. Place in the refrigerator. In a medium bowl, stir together the granulated sugar, lemon zest and juice, salt, applesauce, cornstarch, and baking powder.

Insert the crisper plate into the basket and the basket into the unit.

Preheat the unit by selecting BAKE, setting the temperature to 350°F, and setting the time to 3 minutes. Select START/STOP to begin. Spray a 6-by-2-inch round pan lightly with cooking oil. Remove the crust mixture from the refrigerator and gently press it into the bottom of the prepared pan in an even layer.

Once the unit is preheated, place the pan into the basket. Select BAKE, set the temperature to 350°F, and set the time to 25 minutes. Select START/STOP to begin.

After 5 minutes, check the crust. It should be slightly firm to the touch. Remove the pan and spread the lemon filling over the crust. Reinsert the pan into the basket and resume baking for 18 to 20 minutes, or until the top is nicely browned. When baking is complete, let cool for 30 minutes. Refrigerate to cool completely. Cut into pieces and serve.

Nutrition:

Calories 207

Fat 8g

Carbohydrates: 34g

Protein2g

49.   Baked Apples

Preparation Time: 6 minutes

Cooking Time 20 minutes

Servings: 4

Ingredients:

4 small Granny Smith apples

⅓ cup chopped walnuts

¼-cup light brown sugar

2 tablespoons butter, melted

1-teaspoon ground cinnamon

½-teaspoon ground nutmeg

½ cup water, or apple juice

Directions:

Cut off the top third of the apples. Spoon out the core and some of the flesh and discard. Place the apples in a small air fryer-baking pan.

Insert the crisper plate into the basket and the basket into the unit. Preheat the unit by selecting BAKE, setting the temperature to 350°F, and setting the time to 3 minutes. Select START/STOP to begin.

In a small bowl, stir together the walnuts, brown sugar, melted butter, cinnamon, and nutmeg. Spoon this mixture into the centers of the hollowed-out apples.

Once the unit is preheated, pour the water into the crisper plate. Place the baking pan into the basket. Select BAKE, set the temperature to 350°F, and set the time to 20 minutes. Select START/STOP to begin. When the cooking is complete, the apples should be bubbly and fork-tender.

Nutrition:

Calories 233

Fat 12g

Carbohydrates: 36g

50.   Raspberry Cupcakes

Preparation Time: 15 minutes Cooking Time: 15 minutes

Servings: 10

Ingredients:

4½ ounces self-rising flour

½ teaspoon baking powder

A pinch of salt

½ ounce cream cheese, softened

4¾ ounces butter, softened

4¼ ounces caster sugar

2 eggs

2 teaspoons fresh lemon juice

½ cup fresh raspberries

Directions:

In a bowl, mix well flour, baking powder, and salt.

In another bowl, mix together the cream cheese, and butter.

Add the sugar and whisk until fluffy and light.

Now, place the eggs, one at a time and whisk until just combined.

Add the flour mixture and stir until well combined.

Stir in the lemon juice.

Place the mixture evenly into silicon cups and top each with 2 raspberries.

Set the temperature of air fryer to 365 degrees F.

Arrange the silicon cups into an air fryer basket.

Air fry for about 15 minutes or until a toothpick inserted in the center comes out clean.

Remove the silicon cups from air fryer and place onto a wire rack to cool for about 10 minutes.

Now, invert the cupcakes onto wire rack to completely cool before serving.

Nutrition:

Calories: 209 Carbohydrate: 22.8g Protein: 2.7g

Fat: 12.5g Sugar: 12.5g Sodium: 110mg

Conclusion

U nlike frying things in a typical pan on gas which fails to make your fries crisp and leaves your samosa uncooked due to uneven heat. The inbuilt kitchen deep fryers do it all; you can have perfectly crisp French fries like the one you get in restaurants. Your samosas will be perfectly cooked inside- out. Well, the list doesn't end here it goes on and on the potato wedges, chicken and much more. You can make many starters and dishes using fryer and relish the taste buds of your loved ones.

The new air fryers come along with a lot of features, so you don't mess up doing things enjoy your cooking experience. The free hot to set the temperature according to your convenience both mechanically and electronically. Oil filters to reuse the oil and use it for a long run. With the ventilation system to reduce and eliminate the frying odor. In a few models you also get the automatic timers and alarm set for convenient cooking, frying I mean. Also, the auto- push and raise feature to immerse or hold back the frying basket to achieve the perfect frying aim. So, why should you wait? I am sure you don't want to mess in your kitchen when grilling, baking of frying your food, right? Get yourself an air fryer. Thank you for purchasing this cookbook I hope you will apply all the acquired knowledge productively.

CPSIA information can be obtained
at www.ICGtesting.com
Printed in the USA
BVHW091935180521
607636BV00009B/1148